KNOW YOUR PURPOSE

Unlock the Secret that Empowers You to Be Beautiful, Powerful, and Incredibly Valuable

ANNIE K LAVEN

WWW.TRUEVINEPUBLISHING.ORG

Know Your Purpose
By Annie Kananack

Published by
True Vine Publishing Co.
810 Dominican Dr.
Nashville, TN 37228
www.TrueVinePublishing.org

Copyright © 2025 by Annie Kananack
ISBN: 978-1-962783-98-9 Paperback
ISBN: 978-1-962783-99-6 eBook

Printed in the United States of America—First printing.

DEDICATION

To Sgt. Lynessa VanKirk, a fierce warrior and a beautiful soul who lived her purpose to protect others by fighting for her country.

We will forever cherish and remember her love for us all.

TABLE OF CONTENTS

PROLOGUE

The spacing used in this book is intentional.

It is designed to slow down the pace and ease you into taking the time to listen to your own thoughts.

It is in this space where the magic happens.

So, take your time.

Enjoy the space.

This book is about everything powerful, valuable, and right about you!

Enjoy!

Perspective

Imagine what it would be like if you could know the meaning of your life.

How do you think your life would change?

Would your choices change?

Would your relationships change?

Would the way you feel about yourself
change?

If you knew the meaning of your life, do you think you might have more direction in your choices?

Do you think you might be more deliberate in your actions?

Do you think you might feel more fulfilled?

If so...

Would the effort it takes to know the meaning of your life be worth it?

Would you be willing to take the time to look, I mean really look at your life?

Would you be willing to experience change?

Most importantly, would you be willing to see the most exceptional and lovely things about yourself?

If you are...

then please do continue!

Scan for bonus content or click link below!

https://www.knowyourpurpose.online/perspective

Direction

"Wherever you go, there you are."

To start you on the right path to discovering the meaning of your life, I'm going to state a few facts you may or may not know about yourself.

You are remarkably valuable.

Your life has incredible meaning.

You are capable of discovering that meaning.

You can live an extraordinary life.

So, where do you begin?

How do you find the path to your extraordinary life?

How do you find happiness and fulfillment?

How do you discover the meaning of your life?

Well, you would first need to zero in on where that path will ultimately lead you, right?

In other words, if you are ever going to find your path to happiness and fulfillment, you would first need to know where you are going. And you'd have to be able to recognize that place when you get there.

So, how does knowing the meaning of your life feel?

In that place ...

There is a calmness.

A certainty.

A stable, unyielding, never changing confidence.

When you arrive, it is transformative.

It lifts you out of a random, wandering, rudderless life.

It gives you sparkle.

It gives you direction.

It gives you peace.

We spend our lives searching for the directions to that place.

Do you remember those times when you questioned your choices?

How about when you felt lost?

...or when you felt sad for seemingly no reason?

You looked for something to guide you towards a better place.

What were you looking for?

In your search...

You may have consulted friends,

prayed,

meditated,

worked with a therapist.

You may have even spoken to strangers.

"There has got to be more!" You exclaimed.

And you were right!

You just needed a little bit more direction.

So, how are you going to find that
direction?

You find it from... knowing your purpose.

Your purpose is your home base.

It is that place where everything is right, simple, and peaceful.

It is a spiritual place and purpose is what connects the spiritual world to the physical world we live in.

We can call that connection our Spiritual Fingerprint.

That very moment when you were born, a fingerprint was created and it is that fingerprint that makes you unique. It is that uniqueness that is at the root of what drives you in every area of life.

It is that drive that defines the meaning of your life.

So, if your calling is to spread the word of God, well that is beautiful...

.....and thank you.

But *how* you spread the word is defined by your purpose. It is the very specific impact you create on others that will cause or allow them to listen to your message, instead of maybe someone else's.

Your purpose is a very distinctive gift that makes you unique and is at the heart of how people respond to you.

That is a blessing.

And it's always been there.

You just have to remember it.

Scan for bonus content or click link below!
https://www.knowyourpurpose.online/post/how-to-create-your-best-

future

Understanding Purpose

We've spent our entire lives underestimating the influence of this one word, purpose.

When we think of purpose, we tend to think in vague, unknowable terms and rarely think we are able to actually use it to understand the meaning of our lives.

We use it to describe why we did a particular thing or even to blame someone, "You did that on purpose!"

Today, let's embrace the full expanse of the meaning of purpose by deciding it is possible to understand the meaning of our lives.

Let's start with a standard definition.

Purpose
noun

an intention or aim; a reason for doing something or for allowing something to happen:

Oh, I like that word, intention.

Let's dig a little deeper. Let's define its root word, intent.

Intent
adjective

1: directed with strained or eager attention
: CONCENTRATED

Notice the definition of intent references concentrated.

This gives us a sense of a directed focus.

This means your attention is not scattered or dispersed. It means you are focusing your attention in a specific direction.

You'll also notice the definition references the word, attention. This is the singular form of the word, which means you are focusing on one thing, not multiple things.

Does this mean that at the heart of your own existence there is one overriding intent?...

...One impulse, directed with strained or eager attention?

Yes!

But toward what?

......toward creating a positive effect on the world around you.

How do we know this to be true?

Simple

One can only achieve a positive end goal with a positive intent.

You could never achieve happiness or fulfillment if your purpose was to harm others.

Your purpose is the summation of everything that is right and good about you.

It is light, refined, and simple.

Happiness and fulfillment come from a divine place which makes you inherently divine.

Everything about that is positive!

Everything about that is you.

Scan for bonus content or click link below!

https://www.knowyourpurpose.online/understandingpurpose

You and Your Purpose

There is no one else in the entire world who shares your purpose.

You are special.

You are unique.

You are beautiful.

This means there is no one else on earth who can create the exact same effect on others that you can.

No one.

Do you now understand how important you are to the whole world?

Scan for bonus content or click link below!

https://www.knowyourpurpose.online/you

Forgiveness

There is no reason to get stuck in the wrong or maybe destructive actions or choices made in the past.

They need not define you.

Why?

Because those actions or choices were done without a knowledge of purpose.

They were in fact, to some degree, a result of not knowing your purpose.

Imagine playing a game where there is no clear cut definition of the rules or how the game is won.

Imagine the number of wrong or disastrous moves you would make trying to win that game.

Imagine the number of times you might want to quit.

Am I saying, once you know your purpose you will never make another wrong decision?

No

What I am saying is that once you know your purpose and you are able to put it into words, you will be much more aware of your direction and you may not veer so far off from your path, and it may help you avoid disastrous choices.

Let's recap:

You have a singular intent.

It is positive.

It is unique.

It affects the whole world.

You are magnificent.

Scan for bonus content or click link below!

https://www.knowyourpurpose.online/forgiveness

Orienting Yourself

Here are indicators your life is NOT aligned with your purpose:

Your life feels complicated or jumbled.

You find yourself depressed for no reason.

Your accomplishments feel hollow.

You feel you are accomplishing nothing, despite doing much.

Did one of these describe your life?

If so, you're reading the right book!

Here are indicators your life IS aligned with your purpose:

You can rebound from set backs fairly easily.

You are energized and hopeful.

In general, you are happy.

Your future feels bright.

You are calm and confident.

Did one of these describe your life?

If so, you are living your purpose and now you just need to find the right words to help you use it to build an even more extraordinary and fulfilling life.

Whether you are living your purpose or you feel you are not, the steps to defining your purpose are all the same.

It all begins with understanding the power of words.

And so it begins...

Scan for bonus content or click link below!

https://www.knowyourpurpose.online/checklist

Is It A Goal or Purpose?

Before we get to work on discovering your purpose, we have to make sure we understand that a goal is not a purpose.

This is a crucial point to understand, so let's start with the definition of goal.

Goal
noun

the object of a person's ambition or effort;
an aim or desired result.

You create a goal to overcome something in your environment.

It requires effort to achieve that goal.

EXAMPLES OF A GOAL:

To read one book a month.

To learn how to play the piano.

To work out three times a week.

To plant a flower garden.

To make a lot of money.

To learn a different language.

Goals are those things you set and achieve to expand your abilities in order to get more out of life.

Now that we understand goals, let's define purpose.

Purpose
noun

the reason for which something is done or created or for which something exists.

Your purpose is spiritual.

There is no effort.

It is the horsepower that drives you.

EXAMPLES OF A PURPOSE

To make others feel safe being themselves so they can thrive.

To value the actions of others so they can be confident in themselves.

To empower others' creativity so they can better help the world.

On a daily basis, you create reasons to achieve your goals, but the singular purpose (your primary purpose) behind all those reasons is what gives your life continuity, power, and value.

Your purpose is that unique sparkle in your eyes.

It is that quality that makes your smile yours.

It is you.

Scan for bonus content or click link below!

https://www.knowyourpurpose.online/isitagoalorpurpose

The Purpose of Purpose

Once you have put your purpose into words, what then?

How will you be able to use your purpose to create the most amazing life you know you can live?

Simple.

You can now evaluate every choice, action, thought, etc. against this very specific driving force, which is designed to help you achieve your greatest potential.

It is that potential, when you are able to just be you, that can change the world.

This, in fact, is the purpose of purpose!

No matter how lost you might feel, using your purpose to evaluate your choices gives you a path back to achieving the best life you can live.

Your purpose applies to every area of your life. Every choice you make is intimately connected to your purpose and impacts your overall potential of living your fullest life.

It impacts your career.

It impacts your relationships.

It impacts the way you view yourself.

It impacts the way you treat yourself.

This... is the beginning of everything.

Scan for bonus content or click link below!

https://www.knowyourpurpose.online/challenge

Finding Your Purpose

Before we begin...

I want to acknowledge that it will take whatever time it takes to find the right words to describe your purpose.

You may easily grasp the magnitude of the beauty of you, but some of us learn on a slower curve. It may take longer to allow the words to finally hit home and that is okay.

You might find that you're inspired to read this chapter again and again, and you will find that you will see in yourself things you didn't see the first time.

So, take that time.

It's worth it.

So far, I have given you perspective.

Now, I am going to give you direction.

There are three parts to your purpose:

1. Intention

2. Focus

3. Impact

Part 1: Intention

What do I mean by intention?

For our purposes, it is an action that can't be seen, but can be felt.

Have you ever noticed someone looking at you and you felt something coming from them?

Admiration? Love? Validation?

They weren't saying anything or doing anything, but you definitely felt something coming from them. What you felt was an intention directed toward you.

Now that you understand what I mean by intention, let's get started!

First, you will look for a word that represents that intention you want others to feel when you are near them.

In the beginning, there may be more than one word that feels right, but eventually you'll want to find the one word that captures the effect you most want to create on others.

I've provided you a little assistance on the following pages.

Take your time. Enjoy the process.

Read each of the following words, and apply them to your life. Allow yourself to know what those words mean to others in your life.

If your word is not listed below, keep reading. We approach this step from many different perspectives.

My intention towards others is:

to admire	to respect
to love	to inspire
to accept	to recognize
to foster	to enlighten
to uplift	to motivate
to respect	to appreciate
to welcome	to protect
to promote	to revitalize

to be interested in	to urge
to activate	to validate
to honor	to duplicate
to embolden	to expand
to care for	to illuminate
to acknowledge	to awaken
to calm	to welcome
to strengthen	to guide

Did you find a word or a few words that best describe your intention toward others?

Is there one that speaks to you the loudest?

Is there a word that you hear yourself using?

Is there a word others have used to describe you?

If not, let's look at this from a different perspective.

Maybe you can think in terms of how you make others feel when you are around them.

Others feel treasured?

Others feel believed in?

Others feel rejuvenated?

Others feel seen?

Others feel enlightened?

Others feel renewed?

Have you found the word that best describes the effect you want to create on others?

If so...

Congratulations!

You're on your way!

(At any point you can skip to

Part 2 on page 147)

If you haven't come up with the word yet, that's okay.

Let's try another perspective.

Let's think about this in terms of the gift that you have been given from God.

You might ask yourself...

My gift is to make others...

Feel comforted?

Feel valued?

Feel empowered?

Keep using different words until you find one that resonates.

Still not sure? No problem.

Let's take a look at specific individuals in your life.

Maybe the word will come if you select one person in your life and ask yourself, "How do I want to impact that person's life?"

Need some help getting started?

Here is a list of people you encounter daily:

friends	co-workers
family members	spouse
employees	employer
clients	teachers
strangers	audiences
acquaintances	students
your priest/pastor/ mentor	

Pick one specific person and ask yourself the following question:

How do I want to help _____?

Do I want to motivate them?

Honor them?

Admire them?

Or maybe, do I want to make them feel safe, or feel they belong?

Is there one word that keeps coming to mind?

If you haven't narrowed in on that one word, then continue to do this with different individuals from your list until you start to see a pattern.

Keep going!

You're so close!

Sometimes we can see better through the eyes of others.

Is there a thank you note or an email someone wrote to you?

A recommendation or validation from a friend or co-worker?

If so, read them.

The word might jump right off the page!

If you are not sure you have found the exact right word, repeat one or any of these drills until you feel confident you have found the word that describes your intention towards others and then we'll move forward.

Take your time.

Enjoy the process.

If you find that you have more than one word, and you cannot decide which one best fits, then grab a dictionary and find the definition that best describes your ambition for each word.

You will, once again, discover that the power of the meaning of words will shine through.

Okay! You've found the one word that describes your intention towards others!

Well done! This is a monumental accomplishment!

You could say that suddenly your life has direction!

For some of you, this new insight might bring such joy that you want to revel in the excitement!

Do it!

Enjoy your new perspective!

When you are ready to discover how to refine that intention, join me for part 2.

Part 2: Focus

Now that you have the word that best describes your intention toward others, we can talk about the focus of your intention.

For example:

My intention of inspiring others is focused on what?

Inspiring love?
Inspiring creativity?
Inspiring unity?

Each of these focuses could take you on a completely different path leading you in the general direction of your purpose, but not to your specific purpose.

But to inspire in others something specific, well, that would put you on a very specific path toward your purpose. This would allow you to experience the widest breadth of fulfillment.

So, how do you find the specific focus of your intention?

By asking the question, "what?"

I want to inspire what?
Originality

I want to validate what?
Beauty

I want to appreciate what?
Creativity

I want to empower what?
Spirituality

I want to acknowledge what?
Dreams

Need some suggestions?

On the following pages are listed words that could answer that question, "What"?

Insert your intention into the parenthesis and apply it to the list.

For example...
I want to (inspire) what in others?

I want to ( ) what in others?

brilliance	patience
uniqueness	joy
endurance	stability
intelligence	positivity
strength	trust
commitment	radiance
talent	curiosity
persistence	faith
loyalty	sincerity
happiness	grit

warmth	understanding
integrity	hopefulness
greatness	generosity
success	growth
Integrity	determination
creativity	responsibility
optimism	what is right
kindness	a spirit of play
consideration	empathy
ingenuity	artistry
thoughtfulness	grace
responsibility	peace

Plenty can happen in this section.

You might have quickly found your word.

Your word may not have been in the list, but it came to you.

You might have decided to change your Intention word! That's okay!

Trust yourself!

You are the only one who knows the right answer.

There may be an occasion where your wording doesn't work.

Let's use believe in....

My purpose is to inspire others to believe in....

Well, that's an incomplete thought, isn't it?

In this case, you can again ask, "Believe in what?"

Believe in themselves?
Believe in each other?
Believe in God?

There is a wonderful bonus with regards to focus!

Let's say you realize that your intention and focus, for example, are to inspire creativity in others.

What you will notice is that even those who feel they are not creative, will feel they can be creative just by being around you!

Your purpose is abundantly more powerful than you realize.

If you have a firm grip on your specific intention and focus toward others, great!

If not, that's okay. This next part could be where it all comes together for you.

Part 3: Impact

So, if your intention and focus are to inspire others' originality, it only makes sense to ask the follow up question....

So others can what?

Dream big?

Live their best life?

Expand?

Become curious?

Love themselves?

Help others?

Experience joy?

Accomplish anything?

Realize they are special?

Laugh more?

Follow their dreams?

Heal?

Be free?

Prosper?

Overcome barriers?

Create a brighter future?

This list is infinite.

It is as vast as you can think of things you would want for others.

Here are a few more suggestions...

Thrive?

Get closer to God?

Become imaginative?

Enjoy life?

Trust themselves?

Be stronger?

See beauty?

Find hope?

Achieve more?

Feel special?

Know themselves?

Make better choices?

Be free from fear?

Appreciate who they are?

Help the world?

Believe in themselves?

Make the world a better place?

Follow their dreams?

Rise?

Be themselves?

Create more?

Help others?

Be effective in their actions?

Laugh more?

Prosper?

Think big?

Be more enlightened?

Be comforted?

Did you find your impact?

Great!

Now, let's put it all together!

My purpose is to

_____

(Your intention)

_____

(Your focus)

_____

(Your impact)

Now, take the three parts of your purpose and create a sentence using those words.

For example: My purpose is to inspire creativity in others so they can help build a dynamic and exciting world.

My purpose is to

Wow! You really are beautiful!

Scan for bonus content or click link below!
https://www.knowyourpurpose.online/guide

The Meaning of
Your Life

As all three parts come together, they define just how incredibly special you are.

Your purpose is beautifully powerful. And it is the meaning of your life.

It is you.

v

...and you are all that is good and lovely about life.

Putting words to that loveliness is the kindest thing you can do for yourself.

You can now infuse what's so powerful, valuable, and beautiful about you into every area of your life!

How do you know you have defined your purpose?

Your answer makes you happy.

It gives you peace.

It satisfies the desire to keep searching.

And it inspires you to reach in all areas of your life.

I'll tell you a secret.

My purpose is what drove me to write this book.

My purpose:

To validate what is right about you, so you can be free to be yourself.

What's right about you?

You are beautiful.
You are unique.
You are exceptional.

Your intention towards the world around you makes it a better place.

And...

Your purpose will help the world be that place you've always wanted it to be.

Enjoy this opportunity to experience all that is lovely about you.

You matter.

Your purpose matters.

The world needs you.

I need you.

And I thank you.

One final thought...

Always remember to apply that
lovely purpose of yours to yourself!

Scan for bonus content or click link below!

https://www.knowyourpurpose.online/onlinecourse

www.ingramcontent.com/pod-product-compliance
Lightning Source LLC
Chambersburg PA
CBHW071329120626
46546CB00002B/494